ALL ABOUT
COMMONWEALTH

ANITA GANERI

W
FRANKLIN WATTS
LONDON • SYDNEY

Franklin Watts
Published in 2016 by The Watts
Publishing Group

Credits
Series Editor: Sarah Ridley
Editor in chief: John C. Miles
Series Designer: Graham Rich Design
Art director: Peter Scoulding
Picture researcher: Diana Morris

Dewey Decimal Classification Number: 909'.0971241

ISBN: 978 1 4451 5005 5

Printed in China

Franklin Watts
An imprint of
Hachette Children's Group
Part of The Watts Publishing Group
Carmelite House
50 Victoria Embankment
London EC4Y 0DZ
An Hachette UK Company

www.hachette.co.uk

www.franklinwatts.co.uk

FSC
www.fsc.org

MIX
Paper from
responsible sources
FSC® C104740

CONTENTS

THE COMMONWEALTH

The Commonwealth is a group of 53 countries. It links together some of the world's biggest, smallest, richest and poorest countries, and includes more than two billion people, or around a third of the world's population. Although the countries of the Commonwealth are very different, they all share a common goal – to improve people's lives, education, health, work, surroundings and prospects for the future.

Equal nations

The countries of the Commonwealth range from huge nations, such as Canada and India, to tiny islands, such as Tuvalu and Vanuatu, in the South Pacific. Thirty-two of the countries are small states, home to fewer than 1.5 million people.

The people of the Commonwealth speak hundreds of different languages and follow many different religions and ways of life. Despite these differences, all of the countries are treated as equals. They all support and work towards democratic forms of government, and have similar systems of law and education.

Flags of the Commonwealth flying in Parliament Square, London.

4

Working together

The countries of the Commonwealth share common values and aims – working for peace, protecting people's human rights and freedom, fighting poverty and racism, and dealing with the effects of global warming, drought and flooding. Member countries share their skills and knowledge to help solve problems. Their leaders meet regularly to discuss the challenges facing the Commonwealth, and there are hundreds of joint programmes and projects, linked to health, education, work, law, music, sport and art.

Young people from all over the Commonwealth attended the Commonwealth Youth Forum in Fremantle, Australia, in 2011.

SHARED LANGUAGE

Hundreds of different languages are spoken across the Commonwealth but English is used for official business. The English language was chosen because most of the Commonwealth countries were once under British rule. Having a shared language means that Commonwealth leaders and politicians can communicate easily when they meet.

CoMMonWEaLTH HiSToRY

A stamp printed in Canada in 1898. It shows the countries of the British Empire in red.

The history of the Commonwealth dates back to the time of the British Empire which, at its height, covered about a quarter of the world. Most of the countries in the Commonwealth were once part of the Empire, which means that they were ruled by Britain. This is why English is used as the common language and the British monarch is Head of the Commonwealth. Britain itself, however, has no extra rights or privileges within the Commonwealth.

Early days

In the late 19th and early 20th centuries, some of the countries ruled by Britain began to demand independence. They wanted to run their own affairs. In 1931, the British Parliament passed a law, called the Statute of Westminster, which gave Australia, Canada, New Zealand and South Africa their freedom. These were all countries where British people had settled. They still kept the British monarch but were now equal to Britain, and joined Britain as members of the 'British Commonwealth of Nations'.

MAHATMA GANDHi

Mahatma Gandhi (1869–1948) helped to lead Indians in their struggle against British rule. He believed firmly that non-violent protest was the most powerful weapon that people could use. Instead of fighting, he led peaceful marches and boycotts of British goods. He was often sent to prison by the British authorities.

Indian independence

Meanwhile, unrest was growing in India from the 1880s onwards. The British were reluctant to give up control as India was of great value to them financially and politically. Although large numbers of Indian troops fought for Britain in both world wars, both of the main political parties – the Indian National Congress and the All-India Muslim League – called for India to be able to govern itself. So Congress began a 'Quit India' campaign to force the British out. In 1947, India finally became independent, and part of India became the new country of Pakistan.

Part of a parade marking Indian Independence Day in 1947. India went on to become a very important member of the Commonwealth.

Two years later, India became a republic which meant that the British monarch was no longer its head of state. But India also wanted to join the Commonwealth and agreed to accept the monarch as Head of the Commonwealth. This marked a great change in the organisation. The name 'British' was dropped and the Commonwealth became 'a free association of independent nations'.

Modern Commonwealth

From its British beginnings, the Commonwealth was to become a modern, multi-racial organisation. In 1948, there were only eight countries in the Commonwealth – Australia, Canada, New Zealand, South Africa, the United Kingdom, India, Pakistan and Ceylon (now called Sri Lanka). In 1957, Ghana, in West Africa, became independent of British rule, and Kwame Nkrumah was released from prison to become Prime Minister. Under his leadership, Ghana became the first black African country to join the Commonwealth.

In the 1960s and 1970s, many other African countries became independent and followed Ghana's lead, including Nigeria, Tanzania, Kenya, Botswana and Zambia. They were joined by countries in Asia, the Caribbean and the South Pacific. Soon, the Commonwealth had grown to more than 30 members.

Many students in colleges, such as this one in Ghana, are sponsored by Commonwealth educational projects.

South Africa and apartheid

Racial equality was, and still is, one of the Commonwealth's most important values. It is strongly against any form of racism. In 1961, South Africa left the Commonwealth because of its government's racist policies, called apartheid (meaning 'separation'). Under apartheid, black people were treated very badly, compared to white people. They were kept apart from white people, and had to use separate buses, schools and hospitals. They were told where they could live and work, and had no political rights. Many black leaders were arrested, and spent years in prison.

After years of bitter struggle, apartheid finally ended in 1994. For the first time, every adult South African, black or white, was allowed to vote. A democratic government was elected, with Nelson Mandela (see box), as the country's first black president, and South Africa rejoined the Commonwealth, after a 33-year break. In Mandela's words: "The Commonwealth makes the world safe for diversity."

NELSON MANDELA

Born in 1918, Nelson Mandela became a lawyer and joined the African National Congress (ANC) to fight for equal rights for black South Africans. Together with Oliver Tambo, he set up the first black law firm in South Africa where poor people could come for help. In 1964, Mandela was sent to prison, accused of sabotage and plotting to overthrow the government. He was released in 1990 and helped to bring apartheid to an end. He was an inspiration to people all around the world and was greatly mourned when he died in 2013.

Nelson Mandela's release from prison in 1990 was headline news around the world.

DAILY NEWS TANZANIA

WEDNESDAY, MAY 4, 1994

ANC wins a landslide victory in South Africa, Mandela says

'WE ARE FREE AT LAST'

... Bunge hails Mandela

THE COMMONWEALTH TODAY

Today, the Commonwealth has 53 members. All of these countries, apart from Mozambique and Rwanda, were once part of the British Empire. These two countries were allowed to join as special exceptions to the rule. All members are expected to follow the common goals of the Commonwealth, including working towards world peace, freedom, human rights, equality and free trade.

Children relax and play outside a village school in Bangladesh, one of the poorest countries in the Commonwealth.

United but different

The 53 Commonwealth members include an amazing variety of countries. They range from the world's second largest country by size, Canada, to some of the world's smallest and most remote nations, such as Tuvalu. Smaller countries in particular benefit from the opportunity for their concerns to be considered by world leaders, which is more difficult within much larger organisations such as the United Nations. Commonwealth countries work together, while agreeing to differ on some points, in order to focus on the main aims of the organisation.

DIFFERENT LANGUAGES

In most Commonwealth countries, English is widely spoken and understood. Sometimes, it is a joint official language of the country. But people speak hundreds of other languages as well. South Africa, for example, has 11 official languages, including English, Afrikaans, Xhosa and Zulu. Most South Africans speak more than one language.

Around the Commonwealth, people lead very different lives. In some countries, such as Australia, people mostly live in big cities in modern houses and apartment blocks. In others, such as Papua New Guinea, people traditionally live in small villages in the countryside. Standards of living also vary, from wealthy countries, such as Singapore, with strong economies, to poorer, developing countries, such as Bangladesh.

The Commonwealth is a huge melting-pot of cultures and beliefs. All of the world's main religions – Hinduism, Sikhism, Buddhism, Islam, Christianity and Judaism – are practised, along with many more. Some citizens of one Commonwealth country have settled in another, and taken their culture with them. Acceptance of other people's beliefs and cultures is one of the key aims of the Commonwealth.

Students get on a school bus in Canada, the largest and one of the wealthiest Commonwealth countries.

THE COMMONWEALTH TODAY

Common goals

All Commonwealth countries share a set of common values and goals. These were set down by the Commonwealth Heads of Government. They include good government (based on democracy), human rights (including equal rights) and protection of the environment. The Heads of Government agree to stand by these principles on behalf of their people. If a country breaks the rules, it can be suspended or even expelled, as happened to Fiji after a military coup took power in 2006. Fiji has since been readmitted into the Commonwealth after democratic elections were held in September 2014.

People's rights and freedoms are seen as very important in the Commonwealth. They include civil rights, such as the right to follow the religion of your choice; economic rights, such as the right to a decent standard of living; and social rights, such as the right to an education and fair working conditions.

The Commonwealth flag flies over the Parliament building in Ottawa, Canada.

Commonwealth Day

Commonwealth Day is celebrated on the second Monday in March every year, to mark the work of the Commonwealth. Around the world, special events, parades, lectures and other activities take place, organised by schools, youth groups and governments. In London, a multi-faith service is held at Westminster Abbey. It is attended by Queen Elizabeth II, the Head of the Commonwealth, representatives from the Commonwealth countries and school children.

Each year, Commonwealth Day has a special theme which is celebrated throughout the year. 'Team Commonwealth' was the theme for 2014 seeking to inspire people, governments and institutions to work together for the main Commonwealth aims. The theme for 2015 is "A Young Commonwealth". It aims to celebrate the vital role played by young people at the heart of sustainable development and democracy.

Young people carrying flags to mark Commonwealth Day.

COMMONWEALTH FLAG

The Commonwealth flag has a blue background, with the Commonwealth symbol in gold. The symbol shows a globe, surrounded by a pattern of spears in the shape of a letter 'C'. The spears do not stand for the number of countries in the Commonwealth. They symbolise the many different Commonwealth activities around the world.

HEAD OF THE COMMONWEALTH

In 1949, the leaders of the Commonwealth countries agreed that the British monarch should be Head of the Commonwealth. At that time, the monarch was King George VI. When he died in 1952, his daughter, Queen Elizabeth II, took on the role. Queen Elizabeth is also queen of 16 Commonwealth countries, called the Commonwealth Realms.

Queen Elizabeth II arriving at Westminster Abbey in 2013 to attend the Commonwealth Day service.

Special symbol

The Queen does not have the power to decide what the Commonwealth should and should not do, nor how it carries out its affairs. Instead, she is seen as a symbol of how the Commonwealth countries work together as equals, and as a link between all of its members. When Queen Elizabeth II dies, her heir (Prince Charles) will not automatically become Head of the Commonwealth. It will be up to the Commonwealth Heads of Government to decide what they want to do about this very special role.

COMMONWEALTH TOUR

The Queen's first Commonwealth tour was in 1953–54, soon after she came to the throne. Travelling aboard the Royal Yacht Britannia, the Queen visited Bermuda, Jamaica, Fiji, Tonga, New Zealand, Australia, the Cocos Islands, Sri Lanka, Aden, Uganda, Malta and Gibraltar. This mammoth tour lasted for six months.

Commonwealth visits

During her reign, the Queen has visited all of the Commonwealth countries, apart from Cameroon and Rwanda. She has visited some countries, such as Australia and Canada, many times. Her husband, the Duke of Edinburgh, and other members of the royal family are also regular visitors to Commonwealth countries.

Queen Elizabeth II being carried ashore on a visit to the island of Tuvalu in 1982.

Commonwealth duties

Queen Elizabeth takes her role as Head of the Commonwealth very seriously and is proud of what the Commonwealth has achieved. She describes the Commonwealth as a family, "... at ease with each other, enjoying its shared history and ever ready and willing to support its members in the most dire of circumstances."

The Queen's duties include keeping in touch with the Commonwealth through regular meetings with the Commonwealth Secretary-General and the Commonwealth Heads of Government. Each year, she attends the Commonwealth Day celebrations in London, including the service in Westminster Abbey (see page 13). She also speaks to the Commonwealth through her Christmas and Commonwealth Day messages. These are broadcast to millions of people around the world on TV, radio and the Internet.

Queen Elizabeth II meets people on a visit to Jamaica in 2002.

RUNNING THE COMMONWEALTH

The Commonwealth is an enormous organisation, and thousands of people are involved in its running. Some of these belong to the governments of the member countries, but there are also hundreds of non-governmental organisations spread all over the Commonwealth, working in sport, art, music, health, education, work and law.

Queen Elizabeth II with the leaders of the Commonwealth countries at the CHOGM in Perth, Australia, in 2011.

Commonwealth Heads of Government

Twice a year, the leaders of the Commonwealth countries meet to talk about the challenges facing the Commonwealth, and discuss possible solutions. They talk about world affairs, such as terrorism, and agree a united Commonwealth view on them. Most importantly, they agree the policies and activities of the Commonwealth for the next two years.

At these Commonwealth Heads of Government Meetings (CHOGMs), every leader has the same standing, no matter if their country is rich, poor, large or small. The meetings used to take place in London but are now held in different Commonwealth countries. The last meeting took place in Sri Lanka in November 2013 (see page 25). The next one will take plave in November 2015 in Malta. Each meeting opens with a formal ceremony which the Queen usually attends.

Marlborough House in London is the headquarters of the Commonwealth Secretariat.

Commonwealth Secretariat

The Commonwealth Secretariat is based at Marlborough House in London. Its main job is to carry out any decisions that the CHOGMs make. There are different departments for human rights, youth affairs, economic affairs and so on. The Secretariat decides which areas are to be a priority for the Commonwealth and forms a plan of action for them.

The Secretariat has around 275 staff from many different countries in the Commonwealth. It is headed by the Secretary-General who is appointed by the Heads of Government for a maximum of two four-year terms. He or she is helped by a Deputy Secretary-General who manages the work of the Secretariat and put its programmes into practice.

KAMALESH SHARMA

The current Secretary-General of the Commonwealth is Kamalesh Sharma (born 1941) from India. He was elected at the 2007 CHOGM in Kampala, Uganda, and took office on 1 April 2008. Before this, Sharma was the Indian High Commissioner in London and was closely involved in many Commonwealth activities.

THE COMMONWEALTH AT WORK

The Commonwealth works with its member countries in many different areas, from democracy and trade, to healthcare, human rights and the environment. There are Commonwealth projects and plans of action all over the world, making use of a huge pool of shared skills and expertise to help solve problems and make people's lives better.

Fair government

The Commonwealth works hard to help member countries build strong democracies. Democracy is a form of government in which everyone has the right to vote. In a democracy, there must be regular elections when people can choose their leaders. The Commonwealth regularly sends observers to make sure that elections are held fairly. The observers visit polling stations to check that people are able to cast their votes and, afterwards, that the votes are properly counted.

Commonwealth observers visiting a polling station in Lesotho, Africa, during elections in 2012.

Trading links

The Commonwealth runs many projects to help countries improve their economies. One way is to train farmers in growing new crops that can be sold abroad. In Southern Africa, farmers are being helped to grow organic fruit and vegetables which are in great demand in Europe. Another way is to encourage countries to manage their natural resources better. In the Solomon Islands, islanders receive advice on how to boost tourism to their beautiful home. Trading links between members are also very important, especially for the smaller and poorer countries.

Protecting the environment

Many Commonwealth countries are being affected by climate change. The Maldives is a tiny island country in the Indian Ocean. Today, the islands are in serious danger of being flooded because of rises in sea level, caused by global warming. In Africa, droughts are getting worse; Kenya recently suffered its worst drought for 20 years. Commonwealth advisors help and advise member countries to manage these life-threatening situations.

The Maldives are only about 1.5 m above sea level, putting them at serious risk of flooding if sea levels rise.

RAINFOREST RESCUE

All over the world, rainforests are being destroyed at an alarming rate. In 1989, the government of Guyana agreed to set aside a large area of rainforest as an experiment. Half of the area would stay as wild forest. Half would be run in a way that would benefit people, animals and plants. Working in partnership with local rainforest people, the Commonwealth helped the government to set up a centre to manage the project. It is hoped that other countries will follow Guyana's lead to help protect rainforests for the future.

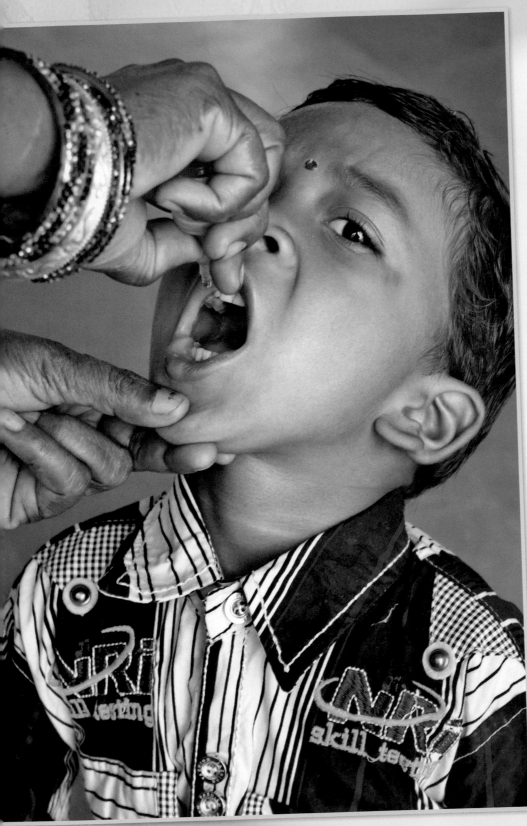

Healthcare

In poorer Commonwealth countries, many people do not have good healthcare. There are not enough doctors, hospitals or medicines. Many children die at a young age from diseases that a simple vaccination could stop. The Commonwealth helps to train health workers and set up clinics.

One of the most serious health problems facing many Commonwealth countries, especially in Africa, is the disease HIV/AIDs. In 1993, the Commonwealth began a programme called Ambassadors for Positive Living. The ambassadors are young men and women who have HIV/AIDS. They talk to other people about their disease and tell people how they can help to reduce the risk of infection.

Commonwealth-trained health workers help to vaccinate Indian children against polio, a dangerous and infectious disease.

Young people

The Commonwealth Youth Programme (CYP) encourages young people (aged 15 to 29) to be actively involved in their country's affairs and those of the Commonwealth. Some countries hold their own youth parliaments where young people can learn more about politics and how democracy works. The CYP also helps young people to fulfill their potential, get an education, find jobs or start their own businesses. One project in India and Pakistan involves vans fitted with computers. They visit rural areas so that young people can learn computer skills.

In some African countries, young people have been very badly affected by devastating civil wars. Some were kidnapped from their villages and forced to fight as child-soldiers. In Uganda, a Commonwealth project is helping them to put their lives back on track. Some have become teachers or doctors; others have set up support groups for young war victims.

A former child soldier in Uganda makes and sells objects from beads to earn some money and build a new life for her and her child.

COMMONWEALTH WAR GRAVES COMMISSION

The Commonwealth War Graves Commission (CWGC) was set up in 1917. It looks after the graves of 1.7 million men and women from Commonwealth countries who died in the two world wars. The Commission cares for cemeteries and memorials in more than 150 countries around the world. The largest cemetery is Tyne Cot in Belgium, with almost 12,000 graves of soldiers who died during the First World War; more than 70% of the graves belong to unidentified soldiers.

COMMONWEALTH GAMES

Competitors racing in the men's 100 metres at the 2010 Commonwealth Games in Delhi, India.

The Commonwealth Games is a huge, international sporting event which is held every four years in a different Commonwealth country. They are known as the 'friendly games' because their aim is 'to promote a unique, friendly, world-class Games, and to develop sport for the benefit of the people, the nations and the territories of the Commonwealth and thereby strengthen the Commonwealth' (Commonwealth Games Federation).

The Games and their history

The first Commonwealth Games were held in Hamilton, Canada, in 1930. Four hundred athletes from just 11 countries took part, and they had to sleep in a local school. Most of the competitors were men. Women were only allowed to take part in a few events, including swimming.

Over the years, the Games have changed in many ways. Today, more than 4,000 athletes take part, and men and women are treated as equals, across all sports. From 1930–1994, only individual events were held. The first team sports (cricket, hockey, netball and rugby sevens) were introduced at the 1998 Games in Kuala Lumpur, Malaysia. The 2010 Games took place in New Delhi, India. This was the first time that India had hosted the Games, and only the second time that they had been held in Asia (after Kuala Lumpur). Glasgow, Scotland was the host for the 2014 Games, while the 2018 Games will be held in Gold Coast City, Queensland, Australia.

Taking part

At the first Commonwealth Games in Hamilton, Ontario, Canada, there were only six sports. Today, organisers must include a minimum of ten core sports, such as athletics, swimming, netball and bowls, and can then add another seven sports from a long list. Events for disabled athletes are held alongside those for able-bodied competitors. At the opening ceremony of every Games, an athlete from the host country takes an oath, promising that all competitors will take part in the spirit of true sportsmanship.

Dancers performing at the opening ceremony of the 2014 Commonwealth Games in Glasgow, Scotland.

YOUTH GAMES

Alongside the main Games, the Commonwealth Youth Games are held every four years for young people, aged between 14 and 18. The first Youth Games were held in Edinburgh in 2000. The next Games will take place in Samoa in 2015. The competition must include a minimum of six and a maximum of eight sports, with no more than two team sports.

23

FUTURE OF THE COMMONWEALTH

In 2009, the Commonwealth celebrated the 60th anniversary of the London Declaration. This was the agreement that allowed India, and other republics, to become members of the Commonwealth, and that marked the beginning of the modern Commonwealth. But what does the future hold for the Commonwealth? Does it still matter in the 21st century or is it an outdated organisation that does not have a place today?

The Commonwealth building (in the foreground) in Colombo, Sri Lanka.

Against and for

Some people have criticised the Commonwealth for not speaking out strongly on its core values, such as democracy and humans rights. They accuse it of not being firm enough with countries where these values are not followed, and of not seeing reforms through. Others say that the Commonwealth has become like an outdated club, based on historical ties that do not count anymore today. This appears to be part of the reason why Gambia's President Yahya Jammeh withdrew his country from the Commonwealth in 2013.

For other people, however, the Commonwealth is still very important. It gives small, poor countries the chance for an equal say with large and wealthy countries. It allows skills and expertise to be shared. In addition, millions of people benefit from Commonwealth-run projects in health, education and so on. And finally, there are still many countries that want to join the Commonwealth family.

Commonwealth Charter

On Commonwealth Day 2013, Queen Elizabeth II signed a charter which sets out the 16 most important beliefs of the Commonwealth for the first time. This had been agreed by all of the Commonwealth leaders as a way of setting out very strongly the Commonwealth's commitment to the future. It brings together the key hopes and values of the Commonwealth – democracy, human rights and fair laws – and opposes "all forms of discrimination, whether rooted in gender, race, colour, creed, political belief or other grounds".

Prince Charles representing Queen Elizabeth II on a visit to New Zealand. He is receiving a traditional Maori greeting.

FUTURE CHALLENGES

Whatever its future, the Commonwealth faces many challenges. The last Commonwealth Heads of Government Meeting took place in Colombo, Sri Lanka, in November 2013. Beforehand, there had been pressure to hold the meeting elsewhere because of the country's poor human rights record. The leaders of Canada, India and Mauritius boycotted the meeting. It was also only the second CHOGM that Queen Elizabeth II has missed. Her son, Prince Charles, took her place.

COUNTRIES OF THE COMMONWEALTH

The boxes below include information about the 53 countries of the Commonwealth, including flags, capital cities and when they joined as members.

Antigua and Barbuda

Capital city **Saint John's**

Area (sq km) **443**

Area (sq miles) **161**

Population **90,156**

Date joined **1981**

Australia

Capital city **Canberra**

Area (sq km) **7,741,220**

Area (sq miles) **2,988,902**

Population **22,262,501**

Date joined **1931**

Bahamas

Capital city **Nassau**

Area (sq km) **13,880**

Area (sq miles) **5,359**

Population **319,031**

Date joined **1973**

Bangladesh

Capital city **Dhaka**

Area (sq km) **143,998**

Area (sq miles) **55,598**

Population **163,654,860**

Date joined **1972**

Barbados

Capital city **Bridgetown**

Area (sq km) **430**

Area (sq miles) **166**

Population **288,725**

Date joined **1966**

Belize

Capital city **Belmopan**

Area (sq km) **22,966**

Area (sq miles) **8,867**

Population **334,297**

Date joined **1981**

Botswana

Capital city **Gaborone**

Area (sq km) **581,730**

Area (sq miles) **224,607**

Population **2,127,825**

Date joined **1966**

Brunei Darussalam

Capital city **Bandar Seri Begawan**

Area (sq km) **5,765**

Area (sq miles) **2,226**

Population **415,717**

Date joined **1984**

Cameroon

Capital city **Yaounde**
Area (sq km) **475,440**
Area (sq miles) **183,568**
Population **20,549,221**
Date joined **1995**

Canada

Capital city **Ottawa**
Area (sq km) **9,984,670**
Area (sq miles) **3,855,103**
Population **34,568,211**
Date joined **1931**

Cyprus

Capital city **Nicosia**
Area (sq km) **9,251**
Area (sq miles) **3,572**
Population **1,155,403**
Date joined **1961**

Dominica

Capital city **Roseau**
Area (sq km) **751**
Area (sq miles) **290**
Population **73,286**
Date joined **1978**

Fiji

Capital city **Suva**
Area (sq km) **18,274**
Area (sq miles) **7,056**
Population **896,758**
Date joined **1970**

Ghana

Capital city **Accra**
Area (sq km) **238,533**
Area (sq miles) **92,098**
Population **25,199,609**
Date joined **1957**

Grenada

Capital city **Saint George's**
Area (sq km) **344**
Area (sq miles) **133**
Population **109,590**
Date joined **1974**

Guyana

Capital city **Georgetown**
Area (sq km) **214,969**
Area (sq miles) **83,000**
Population **739,903**
Date joined **1966**

India

Capital city **New Delhi**
Area (sq km) **3,287,263**
Area (sq miles) **1,269,219**
Population **1,220,800,359**
Date joined **1947**

Jamaica

Capital city **Kingston**
Area (sq km) **10,991**
Area (sq miles) **4,244**
Population **2,909,714**
Date joined **1962**

Kenya

Capital city **Nairobi**
Area (sq km) **580,367**
Area (sq miles) **224,081**
Population **44,037,656**
Date joined **1963**

Kiribati

Capital city **Tarawa**
Area (sq km) **811**
Area (sq miles) **313**
Population **103,248**
Date joined **1979**

Lesotho

Capital city **Maseru**
Area (sq km) **30,355**
Area (sq miles) **11,720**
Population **1,936,181**
Date joined **1966**

Malawi

Capital city **Lilongwe**
Area (sq km) **118,484**
Area (sq miles) **45,747**
Population **16,777,547**
Date joined **1964**

Malaysia

Capital city **Kuala Lumpur**
Area (sq km) **329,847**
Area (sq miles) **127,355**
Population **29,628,392**
Date joined **1957**

Maldives

Capital city **Male**
Area (sq km) **298**
Area (sq miles) **115**
Population **393,988**
Date joined **1982**

Malta

Capital city **Valletta**
Area (sq km) **316**
Area (sq miles) **122**
Population **411,277**
Date joined **1964**

Mauritius

Capital city **Port Louis**
Area (sq km) **2,040**
Area (sq miles) **788**
Population **1,322,238**
Date joined **1968**

Mozambique

Capital city **Maputo**
Area (sq km) **799,380**
Area (sq miles) **308,642**
Population **24,096,669**
Date joined **1995**

Namibia

Capital city **Windhoek**
Area (sq km) **824,292**
Area (sq miles) **318,261**
Population **2,182,852**
Date joined **1990**

Nauru

Capital city **No official capital**
Area (sq km) **21**
Area (sq miles) **8**
Population **9,434**
Date joined **1968**

New Zealand

Capital city **Wellington**
Area (sq km) **267,710**
Area (sq miles) **103,363**
Population **4,365,113**
Date joined **1931**

Nigeria

Capital city **Abuja**
Area (sq km) **923,768**
Area (sq miles) **356,669**
Population **174,507,539**
Date joined **1960**

Pakistan

Capital city **Islamabad**
Area (sq km) **796,095**
Area (sq miles) **307,374**
Population **193,238,868**
Date joined **1947**

Papua New Guinea

Capital city **Port Moresby**
Area (sq km) **462,840**
Area (sq miles) **178,704**
Population **6,431,902**
Date joined **1975**

Rwanda

Capital city **Kigali**
Area (sq km) **26,338**
Area (sq miles) **10,169**
Population **12,012,589**
Date joined **2009**

St Kitts and Nevis

Capital city **Basseterre**
Area (sq km) **261**
Area (sq miles) **101**
Population **51,134**
Date joined **1983**

St Lucia

Capital city **Castries**
Area (sq km) **616**
Area (sq miles) **238**
Population **162,781**
Date joined **1979**

St Vincent and the Grenadines

Capital city **Kingstown**
Area (sq km) **389**
Area (sq miles) **150**
Population **103,220**
Date joined **1979**

Samoa

Capital city **Apia**
Area (sq km) **2,831**
Area (sq miles) **1,093**
Population **195,476**
Date joined **1970**

Seychelles

Capital city **Victoria**
Area (sq km) **455**
Area (sq miles) **176**
Population **90,846**
Date joined **1976**

Sierra Leone

Capital city **Freetown**
Area (sq km) **71,740**
Area (sq miles) **27,699**
Population **5,612,685**
Date joined **1961**

Singapore

Capital city **Singapore**
Area (sq km) **697**
Area (sq miles) **269**
Population **5,460,302**
Date joined **1965**

Solomon Islands

Capital city **Honiara**
Area (sq km) **28,896**
Area (sq miles) **11,157**
Population **597,248**
Date joined **1978**

South Africa

Capital cities **Pretoria/Cape Town/Bloemfontein**
Area (sq km) **1,219,090**
Area (sq miles) **470,693**
Population **48,601,098**
Date joined **1931**

Sri Lanka

Capital city **Colombo**
Area (sq km) **65,610**
Area (sq miles) **25,332**
Population **21,675,648**
Date joined **1948**

Swaziland

Capital city **Mbabane**
Area (sq km) **17,364**
Area (sq miles) **6,704**
Population **1,403,362**
Date joined **1968**

Tonga

Capital city **Nuku'alofa**
Area (sq km) **747**
Area (sq miles) **288**
Population **106,322**
Date joined **1970**

Trinidad and Tobago

Capital city **Port of Spain**
Area (sq km) **5,128**
Area (sq miles) **1,980**
Population **1,225,225**
Date joined **1962**

Tuvalu

Capital city **Funafuti**
Area (sq km) **26**
Area (sq miles) **10**
Population **10,698**
Date joined **1978**

Uganda

Capital city **Kampala**
Area (sq km) **241,038**
Area (sq miles) **93,065**
Population **34,758,809**
Date joined **1962**

United Kingdom

Capital city **London**
Area (sq km) **243,610**
Area (sq miles) **94,058**
Population **63,395,574**
Date joined 1931

United Republic of Tanzania

Capital city **Dar es Salaam**
Area (sq km) **947,300**
Area (sq miles) **365,755**
Population **48,261,942**
Date joined **1961**

Vanuatu

Capital city **Port-Vila**
Area (sq km) **12,189**
Area (sq miles) **4,706**
Population **261,565**
Date joined **1980**

Zambia

Capital city **Lusaka**
Area (sq km) **752,618**
Area (sq miles) **290,587**
Population **14,222,233**
Date joined **1964**

GLOSSARY

apartheid
A form of government in South Africa in which black people were treated as inferior to white people.

charter
A formal document issued by an organisation or society setting out their goals and aims.

civil rights
The rights of people to be treated equally, have a say in how their country is run, and speak out freely.

climate change
The way that the Earth's climate changes over a long period of time because of natural changes and human activities.

democratic
A type of government in which the people of a country have a say and can elect people to represent them.

developing countries
Poor countries that are trying to grow and improve their industries and economies.

elections
When people vote for, or elect, people to represent them in political or other positions.

gender
Being male or female

global warming
The way in which the Earth is getting warmer, largely because of human activities, such as burning fossil fuels (oil, gas and coal).

human rights
The rights of all human beings to freedom, justice, peace, dignity and so on.

monarch
The ruler of a country, such as a king, queen, emperor or empress.

natural resources
Materials that are found naturally in a place, such as good farmland, coal, oil, forests and so on.

policies
Plans of action followed by people, governments, societies and organisations.

polling stations
Buildings to which voters go during elections to cast their votes.

priority
Something which is more important or more urgent than something else.

racism
To treat people differently and be prejudiced against them on the grounds of their colour or race.

reforms
Improvements or changes that make things better.

republic
A form of government in which the head of state is an elected president.

suspended
Temporarily barred from belonging to an organisation, as a form of punishment.

terrorism
The organised use of violence to achieve a religious or political goal.

WEBLINKS

http://www.thecommonwealth.org/ The official website of the Commonwealth Secretariat, packed with information about the Commonwealth, including profiles of each of the 53 member countries.

http://www.youngcommonwealth.org/ A website aimed at introducing young people to the work of the Commonwealth. Take the animated Commonwealth Tour to find out more.

http://www.cwgc.org/ The website of the Commonwealth War Graves Commission, with information about the two world wars, including many personal stories of those who lost their lives.

http://www.thercs.org/ The website of the Royal Commonwealth Society, an educational charity which works with countries across the Commonwealth.

http://www.thecgf.com/ A website packed with facts about the Commonwealth Games.

Note to parents and teachers

Every effort has been made by the Publishers to ensure that the websites in this book are suitable for children, that they are of the highest educational value, and that they contain no inappropriate or offensive material. However, because of the nature of the Internet, it is impossible to guarantee that the contents of these sites will not be altered. We strongly advise that Internet access is supervised by a responsible adult.

INDEX